MW00444954

Walk-Up Music

Walk-Up
Music

Poems by

Paul Watsky

il piccolo editions
by fisher king press

il piccolo editions by Fisher King Press
www.fisherkingpress.com
info@fisherkingpress.com
+1-831-238-7799

Walk-Up Music
Copyright © 2015 Paul Watsky
ISBN 978-1-77169-026-3 Paperback
ISBN 978-1-77169-027-0 eBook
First Edition

All rights reserved. No part of this book may be reproduced in any form or by any means, electronic or mechanical, including photocopying, recording, or by any information storage and retrieval system without permission in writing from the publisher.

Published simultaneously in Canada and the United States of America. For information on obtaining permission for use of material from this work, please submit a written request to:

permissions@fisherkingpress.com

Acknowledgments

Grateful acknowledgment is made to the following publications in which these poems or versions of them have appeared.

Amarillo Bay: "That's The Answer, My Aunt"; *Atlanta Review*: "She Wanted It All For Me"; *Cadillac Cicatrix*: "Memorial Day Split Tombstone"; *The Carolina Quarterly*: "Mort de Seymour," "Santoka Having Visited"; *The Dos Passos Review*: "Dead Cat Bounce"; *Diverse Voices Quarterly*: "Auto-Exegesis": *Ellipsis*: "Spirit Guides"; *Interim*: "Tsunami"; *Interpoezia*: "You Musta Loved It As A Kid"; *Jung Journal*: "Impossibilities," "Patriotic Weekend," "You've Stopped by Helicon for Love"; *Lullwater Review*: "Feel Free"; *Natural Bridge*: "The Absurd: An Invocation"; *Oranges & Sardines*: "Were I A House"; *Permafrost*: "The Boy Who Won't Eat Eggs," "When Late In The Second Decade Of Her Parkinson's"; *Psychological Perspectives*: "I Will Arise"; *The Puritan*: "This Is A Farewell Kiss"; *Rattle*: "Trust Fall"; *Smartish Pace*: "Mother Liked Asking, What"; *Spork*: "Immortality Revoked"; *The West Marin Citizen*: "Two Elegies"; *Whistling Shade*: "Cain's Perfecto"; *Word Riot*: "The Night Before Easter I Rise."

Special thanks to all who have read the manuscript in whole or part, offering encouragement and suggestions, notably Dawn McGuire, Nancy Kangas, Bob Millar, Ellen Bass, Susan Thackrey, Elizabeth Chapman. My family are a constant inspiration, and in George's case an example of dedication to the craft.

Contents

for George, Simon, Clare

Before

The Boy Who Won't Eat Eggs

having known
since pushing two

that we die
never cared

when he couldn't reach
the faucets

without a chair
and still tries

to conserve
his entire future

like something one hand
can hold, or slip

into his pocket,
weighty, cool

its shell

1

My Friend The River

I couldn't love the lower
Hudson, that sprawled indif-

ference of my childhood studded
with sewage outfalls: *In*

your face, kid. You bother
me. And a limp

rubber floated past, *still*
singing (Issa) its icky

ditty. The Truckee's 90-
foot span: white

noise for sleep, a role
model of self-direction

should one flag, song
as from the Key West beach

girl, alone and welcoming
aloneness, too.

She Wanted It All For Me

Mother tended my cuticles with the nail
of her right index finger, pushing
them back as best she could into their half-
moon beds. Males she respected
got manicures and danced merengues.
At ease with digits resembling mouse-
gnawed Jarlsberg, I disregarded
hands as sculptural desiderata. They had work
to do, those hands, and it wouldn't
always be pretty.

I Am Visiting My Childhood

psychiatrist, who's shed of Freudian
neutrality: jovial,

welcoming, larger than
usual and solid like an

amicable cabinet, a ward-
robe that finally unbends,

drops its arm around my shoulders
as we ride the freight

down to street level in an office
building constructed entirely

from dream. Formerly
invisible, a startlingly attractive wife

tags along, spieling
about their marriage, but the dachshund

whose evening walks I ambushed, man
and dog, to steal

companionship, must have expired
at least fifty-five years ago. Here

in our elevator it goes
unmissed as we descend to street

level leisurely, cheerful nuclear
family, descend, descend.

Disorders Of The Child

In those days before beepers my
psychiatrist, deaf to whether

an emergency was going
down, would pick up during

our sessions. *Dr. Luloff.* At least
twelve and usually shut

tight with hate, I always re-
sented the attention gap. Mostly

it was Mother wanting to bitch
at him. *You've got five*

minutes, he'd say, and she'd cut
loose, those aggrieved pipes

wafting, attenuated, across his
desk. Then he'd break

silence, *Time's up,* and cradle
the receiver, a nice, solid black

phone, just like all
the others. Nothing bad happened to

him—and years later she'd re-
mark, her truculence now man

to man, *You know, when some-*
one pushes, you push back.

Mother Liked Asking, *What*

have you accomplished today? And now
to no good end I inquire

it of myself. As if
such questions ever have good

ends. Were I crazy
enough to hale her back from

Hades she'd still deny
her typical accomplishments amounted

to getting conned by
antique dealers and to pissing

people off. Yesterday I pulled
a few weeds and at dinner drank more

than I'd planned. The Giants
won and climbed two

games over .500. Their accomplish-
ment, not mine.

You Musta Loved It As A Kid

In '62, when the Giants lose
Game 7 1-zip to the Yanks, Matty
Alou on third, Mays, who just
doubled, at second, Richard-
son snaring McCovey's barely-
in-reach two-out rocket, I'm still
a New Yorker, midway through
year six with my psychiatrist, still
detesting sports, while I grind
out the embittering
summer as a brokerage house mail-
room pariah, lonely among
high school dropouts who mis-
read dorkishness as scorn.
If my chain-smoking, Rod
Steigerish shrink in rumpled
shirtsleeves were a GM you'd disenjoy
having him renegotiate your
contract after you'd screwed
the pooch for a sub-par
season—my nineteenth
straight so far. *Read*
the sports page, he orders, before
I interrupt, annoyed: read-
ing won't spring me
from solitary. I hate games
of ball—the plague perennial
at Camp Onota....*So you'll have*
something you can talk with
them about. A cure, I argue
back, uglier than

my malady. But that's all
he gives, or anyway all
I get. At first I'm chewing
cardboard: contextless
numbers, trivia, hair-
splitting, arbitrary rules. In July
of '62, however, New York has it
going, what Jung termed
the opposites—Yankees
stampeding 40 games
over .500, and those far
from expansive Mets prat-
falling onto the fourth worst
W/L record ever (40-
120), just behind 1935's
beneath-contempt Boston
Braves. I fake enthusiasm; parrot
newsprint, and, buddy, within a week
the Reynolds & Co. mailroom goes
all smiles.

          Stuck: maintaining
pals requires me for social
prophylaxis to juice myself
each morning with opinions,
scores. And sadly, in these
naïve decades before informed
consent, who knew from adverse
side effects, iatrogenic
consequences? Waddaya
think happens to
an English major's brain
from auditing week in, week
out while Berra and Stengel shout

their surrealist poems across
the Harlem River? Months
bathing myself daily in vicarious
thrills—personalities growing
magnetic, statistics resonant,
suspense replacing apathy—and
baseball like pain
meds overutilized insidiously
takes hold.

That's the answer! my aunt

happily exclaimed, more and more often as
senility advanced, until her brain shut

entirely down. *That's
the answer*, my wife and I

announce to each other and then
we laugh. *The answer* brings

us close—whether it's a typo or a week
of rain.

Mort de Seymour

The less he could walk the more shoes
my father bought. Aside from bank

accounts and a summer house, his estate
consisted of twelve unused pair, boxed in

their original tissue paper. He had small
feet and I was fresh out of simpatico

little old men. So I stacked
his footgear beside the body, where

it lay, jewel-hilted
sword hugging its right flank, and pushed

the boat, his mobile pyre, out onto the water, shoes and
all among the rising flames.

The Night Before Easter I Rise

every hour or less to pee between
nightmares. One of my dead

friends leads me through the vast parking
garage of a southern city, clothes

working themselves loose from my back-
pack. Already far ahead, he dis-

appears when I pause to gather up the rain
pants. I know I'm missing my

plane, but know little else: the hotel's
name, street address, how to retie

my shoe. In a later bad dream I reach
home, to discover my wife never told

me she's leased out our place for a huge
teachers' convention, now winding down, and

I wander estranged among the messy
partiers. If you die

in your dream it's not predictive, such
as when you're on a journey by boat, or

air, or train. That's ominous. And if
you're like a clueless child unable to keep

up with Daddy because you've forgot how
to walk, have entered your late sixties trying

not to think about that all day long, awaken to no candy
baskets, your own kids

grown up, moved away, the sunny world
quietly detached, well, you can go mow

the lawn, since you're not the type
to pray.

Spirit Guides

George slept with a stuffed
parrot and a monkey, Simon with a soft

orange cat bestowed by his maternal
grandma and, thanks to an inspired toss

at the county fair, with a lemony-
yellow bee big as himself. The bee, minus

its deelybopper antennae, lies face-to-the-wall
where it was thrown on piled-up casualties

beyond the playroom pool table,
my wife's once-cherished Lowly Worm squashed

beneath its butt. Neither
the bee's vestigial

opalescent wings nor its jet black rear end
speak to me, not

as when it whispered to the drowsy
Simon, now a helicopter

pilot, about joyous
flight: vistas, the mysterious fulfillments

of hovering, humming, the *whock, whock,*
*whock*ing rotors and the air's

rush. Si moved on, to nurture his feckless
housemate's cat that loves

his room, and communicates by pissing
on his shoe. George these days makes artful

noise. Monkey or parrot, who
wised him up? *Don't be—*

Craarrk!!—a sap. You've got no chops, no
future playing ball, but considering your memory, your

indefatigable mouth, I smell
a meal ticket, m'boy, m'boy

2

Squaw Valley Pan Shot

Morning's nature talk around the parking lot
underscores tectonic

subduction, upthrust
Sierra, batholith crunched against

granite, opportunistic creeks chiseling
valleys down incompatible

substances, white pine that nips
the heels of retreating

glaciers a mere ten
millennia ago this summer. God

knows, my timing
can be rotten but I haven't bought any

ski areas lately. A tank truck slopping
water out its top

crosses under a shut-down
chairlift, switchbacks up

the slope. On my level, shaded
by subdued machinery, all's

comfortable enough. Fescue
tufts. Tiny

white weedflowers. Scattered
pinecones among parched

rocks. The hillside's entrenched
scars validate its graceful

forbearance while an overcast
moves in, maybe with lightning

to torch the woods. When snow
drops by will we experience a few

twenty-foot-deep cycles before the polar
caps completely

liquefy and drain? Mountains couldn't
care less. Grasses

won't lift
a finger. Clouds,

those airheads,
still congealing to clotted

gray, will carry
what they carry—fire if not

water, defunct
covenants if

not
flakes.

Were I A House

and could choose my own
address I'd settle these joists
in Topanga Canyon. For all
I know the place teems with
termites, fire-hazards, earth-
quakes, and industry
assholes. Who cares. I could be
dumpy as a salt
box, weird as an igloo, allergenic
as a horsehair yurt and you'd still
drive miles to pay me
tribute: the Topanga
yurt—so exotic one can't help
but sneeze.

You've Stopped by Helicon for Love

poems? Erato's on break and I'm sub-
bing. Here. I'll sell you this list of her

medicine chest's less noxious contents,
featuring heavy-duty toenail clippers and a broken

comb. Clio won't steer you
wrong. You require lyrics? Don't pass up

my exact account of the park where I ca-
vorted as a child, bull-

dozed long ago for condos. Quite
moving, the bit about a cement

water fountain on which I chipped
my incisor. Basin never

fully drained—tangled
filth constantly circling that silver

titlike thingy Robert Graves
calls a *navel*

boss. I can tell from your close-
together eyes it's gotta be

tinkly little verses. Only
the other day we moved a

poignant one. Ended with
an s.t.d. Overpriced, to be

honest, same as everything
romantic, and wrong

for your complexion. Try us
back in, say, a hundred years.

Shakespeare in Lust: The Poem

begetter begat
shitter shat

scribbler craved immortality
and the tricksy gods

sublimated him
into language durable

as a scoured-out seashell
depersonalized

of its liquidated
inmate then heaved

onto time's gritty shingle
nothing much beyond

an ill-limned front-
ispiece a bequest:

his lesser bed—
provided he who left

the will
was the Will who wrote

and now we reap
a bonus Every-

manly romcom
foregrounding

anima infatuation
with yon paltry noble-

woman who yearns to
strut her ninety

minutes upon the sexist
stage a mimic boy

impersonating Juliet yearns before
goggling cameras and

us and Will in sim-
ulated privacy to

unbind her pale
though perky breasts

repeat re-prate the aroused
bard back

at himself dissolve
his hypothetical

writer's block while
stiffening Shake-

speare's decayed
yet artfully insinuated

long lost quill
whose scratched-

forth phrases
almost

alone
linger.

I will arise and go now, says my brain, but

the right hemisphere stubbornly elaborates a graffito,
the hippocampus perseverates over long-broken toys, and
the amygdala growls.

I will arise and go, now, announces Ego,

though lacks appropriate authority
to distract Id from compulsive masturbation
or Superego from criticizing Id's technique.

I will arise and go—Now!

Yes!! shouts Shadow, *straight to hell!*
Be nice, admonishes Persona.
Partially disrobed, Anima at the mirror peekaboos her hair
        first across one breast then the other.
Let's get moving, scream the Complexes:
        Up!
        Down!!
        Left!!!
        Anywhere!!!!
Yet the Self keeps its door locked.

I'd have arisen and gone, sighs my mind.

Auto-exegesis

Maybe you noticed how my poems, cha-
cha-esque, often make three moves: up

back, and the third's an allegro triple
stutter to the side, or up again. If

they consisted of only two
parts, Mother would have said, *Like*

a behind, would have jabbed
reflexively, mere incidental sar-

casm, no intent to wound deeply.
Still, I could be avoiding her cheap

shots. Freud declared three re-
presents the male

genitalia: penis and balls. So psycho-
analytically speaking I'm a dickhead.

We'd not have got along. Freud wanted
to sport the only dick in town.

Notes On Form

The Passive-Aggressive

must be wily in sub-
verting an objectionable

given: the illtilted gra-
dient of power. Priapic

Samson, unbright, who trusts
that fem Philistine with

the secret of his strength, better
should right off sacrifice

the opposition's queen than
exit a wrathful

suicide. No, forget Sam-
son. P.A.'s keep it

in their pants until
the other, she or he, falls

asleep. Coyote then will send
his sexsnake

questing subtly, and if you
get knocked up…. Shucks,

wasn't me. Overt form has foes. Re-
sist complacency.

The Absurd: An Invocation

O Janus-faced icon of nature's perverse soul O Diamond

Placebo O muse with Alzheimers O

triumph of outlawed imagination of

the involuntary graveside smile of the erect

middle finger waved in reality's ugly puss O queen

of neither or

Apotheosis of the sublime Leveler

of playing fields Bane

of pomposity Confounder of

fools O Groucho

impersonating a physician O

Putin food courts triplanes Hupmobiles blood-

hounds and leeches O

port-a-pots deep in the picturesque

desert O lobsters

on leashes leveraged

buyouts cluster bombs and fucks O what

me worry O don't

leave me with a chimpanzee that bites men's balls O

babies face down in suburban wading pools O Death on

31

a mountain bike O yuletide

pierceings and botox sex

in a dumpster metaphysics full

professors grand muftis Anglican

primates chief rabbis ex-

traverts belly fat catheters sequined

toreros garlic artichokes wormy

cheeses gas balls

exploding Oh

stars

Impossibilities

A sheer cliff. My filament
of path traverses living rock, around
one of whose abutments
I spot an oncoming Siberian
tiger—which blocks my retreat from
the pissed-off Kamchatka
brown bear to my rear. "So
what did you do?" asks
numero dos, from the adjoining
bar stool. What
could I do? The tiger
ate me.

       Which now brings us to
12:30 a.m. and a disorganized
rustling of plastic
in the unelectrified
cabin. Soon as I turn
on my flashlight it
stops. Finding nothing, I go
back to bed. The thrash
of a frenzied wastebasket
liner resumes. This time
my accurately down-
pointed torch reveals brown
eyes—a stock-still
mouse who comprehends
the jig's up, his entire
life and his pre-
decessors' lives having readied
him for this nowhere-

to-run, no-way-to-hide
moment. He can only gawk at
extraterrestrial daz-
zle until I levitate his jail,
transport it outside to the moon-
lit deck, and land that pod
horizontally, open
end pointed at an opaque
meadow.

Too bad I speak no
Rodent, can't eaves-
drop while he mystifies
his cronies with the whole
sick tale.

Cain's Perfecto

for Jules, who shoulda been there

June 13, 2012, a Wednesday night against
the Astros, we're down for one of Matt's trade-

mark gems, especially Houston being nearly
impotent on the road—not that *we're* entitled

to point fingers. But we bust loose early:
10 runs the first five innings to cushion

this kid of 27 who's been a Giant
since '05, his rookie season, making him

our senior player—bright, farmboy strong,
stoic while we saddle him with brutal

low-score losses—1-0, 2-1—and
mediocre W/L numbers—

69-73 through '11—this great
right-hander mostly a nobody outside SF

and Germantown, TN. The competition iced,
your white-bread hurler stands down

from Hulk mode. Adrenaline subsides
during half hours on the bench; focus

ebbs. Pretty soon the erstwhile patsies make
some noise themselves and things get all

messy. Cain just keeps feeding
Houston his Special K's, 13 up through

inning 7, 103 pitches overall, the first sign
he may be tired coming at number 91,

a two-two count on Jordan Schafer,
their leadoff man, who during the fourth milked

ten throws out of Matt before he whiffed. Now
he squares one up toward Triples Alley, deep

right-centerfield, which nobody covers
typically, and the putz has himself at least a double—except

Blanco's abnormally pulled way over and running
maniacally from right gloves that meteor barely

in his webbing, goes airborne, belly flops onto
the warning track, his upturned mitt sequestering

the ball. Cain, usually Guernsey-stolid, shoots
his arms skyward, ruminates momentarily, tips

his cap to Gregor, and K's the next pair,
so far 2/3 of all the Astros aside from

the second frame, where their 4-hole
J.D. Martinez flies to center and Chris

Johnson grounds out 6·3. But
that final batter in the 7th, Jed Lowrie,

who's already hit a hard one to Cabrera,
left, works his count full, which means

an ump's blown call can terminate the master-
piece. Here Cain makes the inning's other

big mistake, pitch 103,
at the strike zone's upper limit,

probably ball four. Lowrie swings.
Misses. 7th inning stretch. By now Cain,

like a python strangling peccaries, has dealt
a full game's worth of pain, and only three

plays, all outfield, have been challenges,
but how much big snake mojo's left

to zap the center of their lineup in the 8th?
Martinez, slumping, consumes a single pitch—

5·3. Brett Wallace, who arrived
in town hitting a gaudy .385,

doubtlessly bored by fanning (full count
in the second, 0-2 in the fifth), looks, and

the gorgon-hurl turns him to stone.
When Chris Johnson, .284, amasses

his third straight infield grounder, Cain's
dealt 114 blows, with Houston's weakest

hitters due up in the 9th. Closing them out
should be academic, if anything's academic

about a perfecto. This time it nearly is—
so long as you believe 42,000+ standing

straight through and screaming soon as Matt
starts his windup represents routine

enthusiasm: foul-out to left, pop-
up in the same sector, and finally, at number

125, a tricky hop from pinch
hitter Jason Castro, .261, to Juan

Arias, brought in late for defense, near
the line at third, and then his interminable pin-

point relay.
Never

before in franchise history, going back
130 years to 1882. Never by

Mathewson. Never by Hubble. Nor
by Marichal. How great is that? Everything's

arguable, pal, about the sport called
since around 1870 America's

Pastime, arguable and subject
to rationalizing bullshit. Next day

an online article rank-orders each
of the 22 big league perfect games,

attaches names: Lee Richmond, Worcester
Ruby Legs, who threw the first one,

June 12, 1880; within a week comes
the second, by Monte Ward, Providence

Grays; then a 24-year gap until
Cy Young, Boston Americans; a fourth,

from Addie Joss, 10/2/1908,
of the Cleveland Naps; and that's it

for the dead-ball era; Charlie Robertson,
April 30, 1922, Chicago White

Sox, disrupts a stretch of almost five imperfect
decades until, drama in spades: Don

Larson, New York Yankees, Game 5
the 1956 World Series against those

redoubtable, loathsome Brooklyn
Dodgers. Comparatively speaking, modern

history's studded with perfectos and though Cain
has a dandy, club vs. club it's laughable

measured against Sandy Koufax,
LAD, throttling the Cubs one-zip

9/9/1965, only two men on base
the whole afternoon, both off snakebit Bob

Hendley, whose sole run allowed, unearned, derives
from a leadoff walk in the 5th and catcher's

throwing error while Lou Johnson was stealing
third. Well, Hendley didn't lose or Koufax

win all by himself. Team-sport perfection
mobilizes many hands, strides on numerous

legs, resides as thought in the mind of God, as
a diamond in the dreams of multitudes.

Immortality Revoked

I never thought he got away with much,
James Wright, not between a breakdown at sixteen,
likely his bipolar surfacing, then booze, that twisted crutch
on which his chronic symptoms perched to preen
their agitated feathers, reiterated to age fifty-three,
when cancer of the tongue shut him up but good.

Now she busts Wright in this workshop: *sentimentality!*
Why are we reading this long-dead clown who stood
witness for bugs, empathized with *old grasshoppers...their thighs
are burdened*, with bitter working-stiffs who drank,
brawled reflexively, finished unemployed, the eyes
of pasture horses he imagined lonely? They stank,
those soppy poems of his, underscored the wasted words
and life. Those golden stones at Duffy's, merely turds.

Your Name on a Grain

of rice. Most generous
offer so far this
morning: clearly

beats wallowing in my
motel bed, caressed
by Santa Monica Blvd.

traffic noise. For a minor
cash consideration I receive one
rice grain imprinted with

my signifiers—suitable
for purposes of self-
aggrandizement or nutrition. I'm

taking some time to mull that
proposition, on a nice bench
here at the pier, ocean

waves beaching themselves beneath me
without a single grain of
rice to their names.

Tsunami 2011

Hokusai demonstrated that any Great Wave
worthy its name needs something more

than crass dynamism, when he made his Kanagawa
exemplar so splendidly clean—the crisp

blues and whites of nautical dress
uniform—and sculptural, with snow-

capped Fujiyama's background
triangularity pulling together

his 1826 composition. The Sendai seawall
event by contrast resembled Uncle's filth-

laden gut spilling
over his once-neat leather belt, bathetic like

the denouement of Midway, another Imperial
project scripted to illustrate Murphy's

law. Downright ugly: salting the tidy
fields, then harrowing them with

new-minted rubbish—every constituent
of civilization broken down into toxic

sludge stippled with drowned cars and busted
ships—an image to ban from one's trashed

living room to spare
the honored guests.

3

Xmas Card To My Dead

Please forgive the bulk
mailing: Season's Greetings just

for you who've crossed
over or, due to mal-

feasance/manifest
apathy, been dele'd from

that dwindled cat-
alogue of the credit-

able still alive. Happy
New Year if you're de-

servedly in hell. And even hap-
pier if mistaken identity led

to a false con-
viction. I'm petitioning

God to recheck the evidence
locker for your physical

DNA. Should you receive
this missive while yet

animate, don't feel un-
equivocally obliged to go

fuck yourself. I could have
erred about your character, be

acting irrationally
vindictive, even lashing

out in shame at my own
prior misconduct. Oh,

you dear cadavers, every possibility
remains open—except

revenance in the original
flesh. To all those

missed, and those merely
recollected: Peace.

When Late in the Second Decade of Her Parkinsons She Falls

she smiles, or refuses
to cancel the prior

moment's smile
and indulge fall-

ingness, that froward
inner child who casts

down its blameless
doll. Patient, she pains-

takingly repositions
the incarnate self upon

her own two feet, often
having heard *Cowboy*

up! There's no free
lunch (compared to what

your baby brother gets).
Cowboy up, indeed.

Memorial Day Split Tombstone

No Giants game scheduled, so lucky   wife catches up on Tivo'd hard-to-solve
capital crime docs, graphic   evidence galore: bloodstained carpet,
charred skeletal debris, high impact   defiled corpses. Far from sadistic, she

says for her it's all about reassuring   messages, not commonplace real-life
outcomes where scatheless   in a smokescreen of eviscerated tripes the perp
absconds, unavenged strewn victims everywhere   My holiday observances include

freelancing an anti occasional poem, provoked   by a front page, bonus color
photo foregrounding Mary McHugh   in short black sundress, face-down near the foot
of her Iraq-casualty fiancé's   grave. Bare calves caressing, heels

beckoning skyward, America's no   frills prima ballerina propped
on her elbows displays fetching shoulder   blades while lesser dancers, playing head
stones, deploy upstage in ranks, their vanishing   point the cemetery's left

corner. Will this   forlorn sylph, I ruminate off-message, end her years
a spinster? Must I   cast a less girly dame to haul us home from our endless
bungle? Not Ms.   Condi who lied us in. Not the always-looking-out-for

48

#1 Hillary. Nor even undermuscled Nancy P.
Motivationwise, we need Kid-
do, samurai swordfighter complete
with endearing monicker, who, evil
doers aswarm, slashes through
two flics, Xing-out the hit man/boss/
lover who knocks
her up before the opening credits, then on camera shoots
her in the brain. She's tough
enough to offset her loony impetuosity when sword high
Kiddo charges a trailer
trash bad guy's front door straight into tit-high paired
shotgun barrels of rock
salt and winds up buried alive. Flashback
to China: her nasty
advanced training by a misogynistic Caucasian-despising
dandy. This berobed old beard
stroker demands the movie star assault
a thick board till her crippled
hands can't manage chopsticks, but hotcha!
he's infusing her with the essential skills to bash
out of a coffin, scramble up from
dirt, pluck her detestable
female rival's surviving eye, demonstrate the Master's
secret exploding-heart technique on ohsobad
Bill, and toward sun-
rise drive off with her newly-fatherless cute
as-a-bug four-year-old
daughter. Not very pricey, all things told, for un
interrupted peace.

Leveler

There weren't many parts
to an elevator operator's job

in the fancy building just off
Fifth Avenue but a big one was talking up

the weather maybe thirty times
each shift: role-

appropriately, e.g., no
rage or

profanity, no despair. Weather
equalized rich/poor, brought

us together in peace. And whatever
else one might want

to say about a hot, muggy morning it treated
everybody alike out there on

the street until some of us caught air
conditioned cabs.

Monday's Angels

pimp for man-
agement: chivvy
the recalcitrant school-
child, herd blue
and white collars onto sub-
way platforms—
God's Pink-
ertons, they pee
on us and call
it rain

Patriotic Weekend

July 3

For infants the world's a loaded
diaper, for geezers a streetcar
with slashed wicker seats that everybody

takes into the fire, across
the waters, out of the ICU,
face covered with a sheet. And

America's Empire, almost seventy
years down the track from its most
recent glory, shifts foot-

to-foot, one hand in
its pocket, jingling
the tokens.

II
July 4

Evening sun drains from
the treetops in windless
suspension between day
and night. I have paid

my visit and returned to solitude,
nothing but diffident
mosquitoes for company. We're
OK, we bugs, enjoying

our moment as if the clear weather, this
waning commotion for liberty,
personal initiative, were solidly
anchored to a universal slab,

rather than one fictitious point in
a decaying orbit. Today's deal,
and I'll take it. The black
hole can wait,

Santoka Having Visited

the station and seen them off-
loading soldiers' cremains from

China finished
life on his own

terms Oct. 1940 after decades spent
trying

to die: fell
asleep as usual drunk and never again

witnessed the tea
blossoms of dawn or what Japan

summoned onto its own
turf. Sake

his favorite koan got him
in trouble and then got

him out before the bent
nail of his personality

was pounded
flat. He left

behind that image
of Mom's self-

drowned body retrieved
from the family well when San-

toka was eleven. Left his
poems. And sake's still

here for who-
ever wants it.

Feel Free

to visit the isolation cells, suggests
our guide, finishing off the Terezin
Small Fortress tour. After crossing
the Fourth Yard I solo down
corridors of unpadlocked
wooden doors agape on minimal
dry rooms, empty except here
or there a roughly-slatted bed
frame. No more torture
business, not a single zealous eye to
squint through gratings at long-
squandered undesirables. The main gate's
restored *Arbeit Macht Frei*
paint clarifies why these physically
insignificant holding pens became
prisoners of their own dusty idleness.
I move along, a bit early
for the Ghetto Museum.

This Is A Farewell Kiss, You Dog, Shouted

a bellicose journalist later beaten by cops to the tune
of broken ribs, an arm, and internal bleeding although his

family denies he did anything
wrong. Bronze-colored and sprouting

seemingly live vegetation, the large
fiberglass shoe, a sculpted

*source of pride for all
Iraqis,* has been seized on the orphanage grounds

where it was erected, dismantled
and destroyed. *Children should be put away,* Deputy

Governor Abdulla
Jaballa told reporters, *from any political-*

*related issues…since this monument can instill
things*

for which the time is not now. Zaidi, before—worst
Arab insult—hurling

with startling speed and accuracy for an amateur his footgear
at the presumptive Bush, and facing if

convicted up to 15 years, also yelled, *This
is the end.* Yesterday

in Tikrit Shahah Daham informed the German
news agency DPA *I did*

*take the shoe down immediately and destroyed it
and I did not ask why.*

Two Elegies

Szymborska's Ciggies

"I've never been to this part of the cemetery"
from "Funeral," translated by Joanna Maria Trzeciak

Who so pure she craves nothing
to sidle past Hitler, to out-

last Stalin, to cast off what's
left of the here-

and-now? Unlikely she
played ingrate, rebuking

as *cancer sticks* such ever-
loyal hand-

maidens, who cooled her
image through corrosive

decades, cooled her jets, cooled
her out of sight, who long

as they could refrained
from dunning her with

ambulance or hearse, for-
bore while she devised those

perpetual motion mechanical
dolls, her poems,

and set them to dancing
on her grave.

2.

Couple Days Ago They Caught

up with Colonel Kha-
dafy in his improv

hometown hideaway, a
culvert. Already

wounded, that brave man begged for
mercy but too

bad: the crowd finished
him off. It's no picnic

getting old even when you seem
innocent of crimes against hu-

manity. The inevitable
sniffs you out either

down your drain-
pipe or puttering

fancy golf carts around
the grounds of a gated

geriatric reservation. No
more mulligans

for you, Mack. The
end.

Disappeared, Verb, Transitive

for Nadezhda Tolokonnikova

When the world's most power-
ful man's a sociopath.... No! Be

ignorant. Ask cluelessly, *To which
world's powerfulest man might*

the poet refer? Only communicate
in code, so that next morning

you'll find yourself where you went
to sleep, undrugged,

unpinioned, unthrashed,
uninterred in an un-

marked pit. Mustn't
channel any pussy-

rioter, any accidental
nonexistent locutions, any

nobody who repetitiously
blurts prison com-

plaints, then like a dropped
call goes missing (its own

message) in transport to else-
where. Whether such person

receives her Ural mountain
burial or resurfaces in another

jail hardly matters: greatness,
that Putin among mortals, has lit

her into a night flare warning us
the bridge is out.

Well, That's Over

I don't want to be into jihad no more.
Colleen LaRose, aka Jihad Jane, at her sentencing, 1/6/14

I've been at one with
the great ox-

ymorons: love/hate, peace/
war, holy/shit, a real-

time ancient Mayan
priest offering

up hearts by handfulls to
revivify the city's drought-

tinged maize plots. Yowee!
Those circuits were hot,

man. But that was last
year. Now I acknowledge

fallings apart, my-
self shrunk in my peels,

my orange jump-
suit, who'll sing for

a dime, and walk
in four, wist-

ful, clutching
her half loaf.

Dead Cat Bounce

Something's off, I know, about retooling
taxidermied felines as remote-

controlled model aircraft—
abominable, actually, to impose that

on the self-effacing moiré, Lady—
shy, dainty—a favorite of my wife's,

who ran off permanently to cohabit with
distant neighbors after my critters and

I moved in. But other pets might *appreciate*
going Borg, say those adopted

Persianesques, Saruman, his consort Baby
Rosco, and their neurologically

challenged dumb-but-loving daughter
Purrbody, who I found laid out

stiff as a boogie board under
the cabin when she was about two,

most likely head-kicked by a goat against
whose hind leg she rubbed once

too often. Saruman ruled, stole
whatever he craved, and died ignominiously from

pneumonitis. Baby Rosco was a pirate, ag-
gressively territorial, great in skirmishes,

a survivor of everything except her prolapsed
rectum. What a tidy squadron:

he the stealth bomber, huge, black,
and hairy; the Mrs. an AH-64D

Apache Longbow helicopter—belly-
mounted 30 millimeter Chain Gun, Hell-

fire missiles and Hydra 70
rocket pods. I'd compensate

Purrbody's spazziness and fits by
hybridizing her with the agile Lockheed

Martin F-22 Raptor,
a single seat fighter capable

of mach 1.82 in supercruise
mode, whose faulty oxygen feed

wouldn't compromise an already lifeless
pilot. Goats, you got it comin.'

Victory Parade

When your rival, who leads the Series
three games to one, is batting
with two aboard, two out, top of the seventh
in a scoreless duel, first base open,
a 2-0—i.e. home run hitter's—count on
the Giants' veteran 8-hole guy (next man up
their notoriously unproductive improvised
DH), baseball wisdom dictates, *Walk*
Renteria! Don't give that superannuated
prick the slightest
chance to bury you. But this
is Macholand, Texas,
"invincible" Cliff
Lee throwing, and the Rangers commanded by
a players' manager disinclined
to interfere. So destiny
contrives that number 33 uncork the only
pitch our patient batter,
sensibly awaiting his base
on balls, happens
to be looking for: cut fastball
up in the zone, and glorybetoJesus right
down the middle of home plate… If Edgar,

age thirty-five, dreamt of tenderness in these
his senior playing years,
the truncated, soon-to-be history 2010
season (71 games, 240 ABs)
urinated on this humble prayer, heaping
injury atop insult—three visits
to the 14-day DL: April
(groin strain), May (right hammy), August

(strained left bicep, that ruptured and paradoxically
ceased hurting). In September he was day-to-day with elbow
inflammation. San Fran's home
opener shortstop (going three-for-five—
single, double, two-run jack),
Renteria mostly rode
the bench, making the post-
season roster only because Sandoval, our
gluttonous Soph at third, grew too fat
to field and Fontenot, his backup, executed
worse, which persuades Bochy, the skipper, to slide
Uribe westward and gamble on his rickety, over-
priced, they say, Colombian. Luck

hadn't fully blessed the orange and black for almost
six decades. Take
'93: SF wins 103, Atlanta 104. This
past July we sweep
the Mets, except Ishikawa's walk-off
run gets erased at home by an egregious
blown call. August 25, Coors Field, down
by nine we rally to lead
11-10, and lose in 12. Who'd
figure August 26, it finally stops being our
turn to screw the pooch? Hardly
anybody sane. Nonetheless,
San Diego, 6 ½ ahead,
launches the longest
losing streak—10 games—by a first-
place team since Philly in '64.
Last day the regular season J. Sanchez not
just shuts the Padres out 3-zip to clinch
the west, he triples leading off the third, a power
hitter's (which he ain't) gorgeous liner to right

center, deepest corner of the park, setting F.
Sanchez, second basemen, up to drive
him and the division in. Throughout October we
reap a cornucopia of opposition
errors—Atlanta's inept Conrad takes
his starring bow—and downright
eerie gifts. Credit near-
incomparable pitching all
you want, The Force (and I'm not only talking
double plays) was with us: Series Game
2 scoreless in the fifth, Ian Kinsler on
second with a leadoff two-base hit never
advances, thanks doubtlessly to Matt
Cain, but that's after
Kinsler utterly crushes
one to straightaway center where
it bounces backward off the literal fence-
top into play and right at Andres

Torres, whose strong throw pins
that Ranger down
to die.
        The Beard, SF's young
closer Brian Wilson, considered an intelligent
maniac, ditches his official ride, a semi-
private motorized cable car, white name-sign
on its roof, and gesturing vigorously to incite
the crowd, guessed by police at 200
thou to a million, strides
up McAllister toward City Hall. Renteria,
the Series MVP, whose 12th inning single
back in '97 won it all for Florida, shadowy,
quiet within a similar clownish vehicle, rolls
through ecstatic screams.

At Evening I Rededicate My Life

N. Beach, Pt. Reyes, 6/29/'13

Yesterday a river today an
ocean and 7 suns past the sol-

stice that brave boat the body sails
onward while that timid boat

the body quails and wrings its
hands. *What about*

storms, leaking, incompe-
tent crew? Who among those

surviving friends could offer
a tow back to port? The brave

boat chuckles. *If you didn't fall*
downstairs this afternoon why

should you leak? Beside
laughter the material world

wields no literal weapons against
weak metaphors, so even timid

little boats can through self-
assertiveness prevail. Cheer

up. In company we'll cleave
seas of rhetoric like the two sides

of a coin.

Afterward

Trust Fall

There is no scientific evidence…the game builds any trust among participants.
Wikipedia

This exercise must be vol-
untary. It's impermissible to trust-

fall somebody else, like God
did Job—shoved him arsy-

versy onto a shit
pile then garnished the poor

sap with boils. Not,
we hope, Yahweh's signature

moment, and not to be repeated
alone at home with your baby

sister, as in, *Don't*
trustfall little Trudi without strict

parental oversight. No
defenestrations either! It's

different to meetup with cooperative
adult friends and trust fall each

other sequentially, standing
straight, feet on floor, arms

crossed over chest, then top-
pling backward (deep

breath) onto ex-
pectant sup-

port. Aaah! (sigh) How
reassuring one's universe. Let's

do it again, higher, stage-
dive the pulsating cosmos. Soon

we'll be ready to trust that
gravity will relent, and human

nature. Old age retreats
beyond recall as we trust-

fall into harmonious
white light.

Also by Paul Watsky

Telling the Difference
ISBN: 978-1771690263

About the Author

A native of New York City, Paul Watsky moved to California during the late 1960's, where, after teaching for five years in the English Department of San Francisco State University, he trained as a clinical psychologist and Jungian analyst. Paul's first book of poetry, *Telling the Difference* was published by il piccolo edition in 2010. His haiku, longer poems, and translations have appeared widely in periodicals and anthologies, including *Modern Haiku, A New Resonance: Emerging Voices in English Language Haiku, Rattle, Interim, Smartish Pace, Asheville Poetry Review,* and *The Carolina Quarterly*. He is cotranslator of *Santoka* (Tokyo, PIE Books, 2006), and poetry editor of *Jung Journal:Culture and Psyche*.

il piccolo editions is an imprint of Fisher King Press.
Learn more about many other worthy publications at:
www.fisherkingpress.com

CPSIA information can be obtained
at www.ICGtesting.com
Printed in the USA
FSOW01n1245100315
5561FS